BELONG TO

....

....

....

Please take a couple of minutes to leave us a Review and Rating !!!

Thank you and good Luck !

www.ingramcontent.com/pod-product-compliance
Lightning Source LLC
LaVergne TN
LVHW061738250225
804528LV00007B/736